Everyone Loves ELWOOD

A True Story

by

Karen Quigley

with
Loren Spiotta-DiMare

illustrations by
Kay A Klotzbach

Special Thanks To

John Micklewright who saw something wonderful in Elwood and brought him into my life.

Kris Banks who insisted that I enter Elwood in the World's Ugliest Dog Contest making all this possible.

My grandmother who shared her love of animals and the very important message to "be kind to animals".

My Dad who had faith in me and this project.

Loren Spiotta-DiMare whose generosity and guidance was invaluable.

Kay Klotzbach whose incredible art and sense of humor brought Elwood's story to life.

My friends who encouraged me along the way.

All the people who work in shelters, rescues and sanctuaries trying to make a difference in the lives of animals.

But most importantly to Elwood who has made my life more beautiful than I could have ever imagined.

This book is dedicated to the millions of homeless, mistreated and lonely animals just waiting for someone to love them unconditionally. May they find their forever homes.

Save a Life! Make the next member of your family an "adopted" animal.

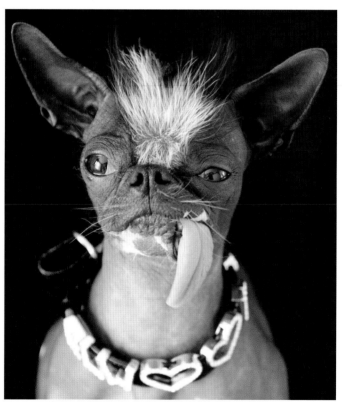

Be Kind To
Animals
Love Elwood

A percentage of proceeds from all sales of this book will benefit homeless and abused animals.

Even as a young pup, Elwood was. . . well, different. He had no fur except for a few tufts on his head and tail. And, his tongue hung out the side of his mouth. The other puppies in the litter felt sorry for Elwood. Even his owner thought he was too ugly to sell and she didn't want him.

What would become of poor Elwood?

Luckily, a nice woman named Mary said she would take Elwood. So the ugly puppy went to live with a whole bunch of other little dogs.

After a few weeks, Mary realized she had made a mistake. She had too many dogs and couldn't take care of them all. Elwood had to go. The funny-looking puppy was very sad. He couldn't understand why no one wanted him.

It was Elwood's lucky day when SPCA Investigator John showed up and told Mary he knew someone who would *"love"* Elwood forever. Her name was Karen and she already had other dogs with special needs.

As soon as Karen met Elwood it was love at first sight. Karen had never seen a dog that looked like him, but she didn't care. To her, he was the most beautiful dog in the world! She brought him home to live with her and lots of other wonderful dogs and cats.

Elwood and Karen started to form a very special bond. The ugly puppy seemed to know his new *person* would love him forever. They went everywhere together. No matter where they were, people would stop them and comment on Elwood's looks.

Sometimes they had nice things to say like, "He's so cool," "Check out that Mohawk," "He's really cute." But not everyone was kind. Some people called Elwood "ugly." Karen understood that people didn't mean to sound cruel. It was just that most had never seen a dog that looked like Elwood.

Elwood didn't seem to mind what people said.   In fact, he was always happy to meet everyone.   As far as he was concerned, he was **very handsome**. He knew this to be true because every day Karen would say, "**Elwood** is sooooo handsome!"

Elwood noticed that no matter who he met they would smile and laugh and just feel good when he was around. He thought, "I must be very special to make everyone so happy." He even heard someone call him *"magical"*, which really made him feel good.

One day a friend called Karen and suggested she enter Elwood in the World's Ugliest Dog Contest. At first, Karen said "No, Elwood is NOT ugly." But then she decided entering the contest might be fun and give them a chance to meet other special dogs like Elwood.

Karen & Elwood Quigley
2002 Special Dog Ave.
Dogs Rule, NJ 08007

TO: WORLD'S UGLIEST DOG CONTEST
SONOMA MARIN FAIR
175 Fairground Dr.
Petaluma, CA 94952

Fragile - Handle with Care

Before Elwood knew it, he was on television shows and newspapers were writing stories about the local dog who was trying to win the Ugliest Dog Contest. His photograph even appeared on the front page of several papers. Soon Elwood couldn't go anywhere without being recognized. He was becoming a *STAR*!

Every day people asked Karen about Elwood. When they were out together, passersby would stop and ask, "Isn't that the dog on television? He's in the Ugliest Dog Contest. . . right?" Strangers wanted to meet him and take his picture. All the attention surprised Elwood but he enjoyed every minute of it.

People still called him "ugly" or said "he looks like an experiment gone wrong". Some people even thought he looked like a "monkey". But Elwood ignored them.

He knew he wasn't any of those things. He knew Karen *loved* him so much. He knew he was very special and all that mattered was he had a loving family and *HE* made people *SMILE*.

M eanwhile, Karen and Elwood had to prepare for the contest. They had to fly to California from their home in New Jersey. Elwood was a little nervous about flying in a big plane, but he knew as long as Karen was with him everything would be OK.

S o off they went to the airport in a chauffeur driven limousine. "WOW" Elwood thought, "I'm getting famous." People at the airport couldn't wait to meet Elwood. Everyone clamored around him wanting to meet this unique dog and have their picture taken with him. Elwood couldn't believe he had his own *Fan Club*.

Meeting all these strangers was fun but *exhausting*. It was a relief when he and Karen got on the plane. Finally, a chance to rest. Elwood curled up in Karen's lap and fell fast asleep.

Finally, they arrived in California. Within hours camera crews for the Animal Planet television show were filming Elwood in preparation for the big contest. Elwood started to meet the other contestants: Lucille Bald, Pee Wee and Jake. The best part was they all looked a little funny just like Elwood! And they all became good friends.

Elwood couldn't believe all the fuss people were making over him. . . and the fun was just beginning.

The day of the World's Ugliest Dog Contest arrived and Elwood was ready. They began with an appearance on a morning television show, followed by several photo shoots with professional photographers, then interviews from television reporters from all across the country, even as far away as Japan and Germany.

Elwood was overwhelmed by all the media attention but he shined every time the cameras were filming. Before he knew it his name was called and it was his turn to meet the judges.

"Oh my," he thought. "Do I have what it takes to be crowned *the World's Ugliest Dog?*"

The crowd cheered Elwood on and he did his best to show the judges his special qualities, like his tongue hanging from the side of his mouth, his Mohawk and his polka dotted body.

Then Elwood heard the announcement, "Now for the winners. . . second place in the mutt class goes to Elwood." Elwood and Karen were so excited. Second place was *great!* Everyone especially Karen was so proud of him.

Elwood didn't care whether he won or not. He had fun, he made new friends, and he made people smile, laugh, and feel good. Then Elwood heard Karen say, "Elwood, you'll always be the *most beautiful dog* in the world to me!" And that's all that really matters.

Elwood's story doesn't end here. After Elwood won second place he spent much of his time helping homeless animals. This made Elwood think, "Maybe I should enter the Ugliest Dog Contest again. If I win I could really help lots of orphaned animals". So the next year, Karen and Elwood went off to California to give it one more try.

Elwood always believed in himself and just knew he could **WOW** the judges this year. He decided to use his charming personality to win the crowd over and the judges too.

Then they announced, "First Place in the Mutt Class… Elwood"; then he heard his name again "Ugliest Dog of 2007… Elwood"; and before he knew it he heard, "Now, for the grand prize of World's Ugliest Dog… ELWOOD"! The crowd went crazy chanting "Elwood, Elwood". Karen and Elwood just couldn't believe it. This little pup stole the show!

Elwood knows that being #1 means he has a responsibility to help others. He hasn't forgotten what it was like to be the pup no one wanted. But Elwood always believed he was TOP DOG and that he would have a fabulous life even though it started out a little uncertain. And what a *FABULOUS LIFE IT IS!*

Epilogue

Elwood continues to fascinate people wherever he goes. He has become a Good Will Ambassador for homeless animals and those with special needs. He uses his celebrity status to bring attention to the millions of animals in shelters and rescues that are just waiting to be adopted and have a fabulous life too. And, to remind all of us to be kind and tolerant of differences.

To learn more about Elwood go to www.EveryoneLovesElwood.com.

An avid animal lover, **Loren Spiotta-DiMare** is the author of three pet reference books for adults and six picture books for children. Her work has been recognized by the Dog Writers Association of America, Humane Society of the United States, and the Doris Day Animal Foundation.

Kay Klotzbach received her B.S. in Art Education from Moore College of Art & Design and her M.F.A. in Visual Art from Vermont College, Norwich University. She has exhibited her work regionally and nationally in a variety of venues. Exhibitions include Penn State University, the New Jersey State Museum, The University of Virginia, Westbeth Gallery, NY City, Delaware Center for Contemporary Art, Wilmington, DE, Rutgers University, Camden, NJ and the Anchorage Art Museum. She has received two Geraldine Dodge Fellowships and awarded residencies at the Vermont Studio Center in Johnson, VT and the Virginia Center for Creative Arts in Sweetbriar, VA.

Kay is an associate professor of painting and drawing at Camden County College in Blackwood, NJ. She is a resident of Lindenwold, NJ where she resides with her husband, cat and three dogs (two of them greyhounds). This is her first foray into book illustration. For additional information please contact kayklotzbach.com.

About the Author

This is **Karen Quigley**'s first children's book. She was so inspired by Elwood she wanted to share his story and his message with children. Karen believes if we are ever going to see a day when there are No More Homeless Pets, we need to teach our children about compassion, being kind to animals, and that all animals and people are beautiful, even the ones who look a little different. A kind heart toward animals is a kind heart toward people, and that can only make our world a better place.

Karen has been an animal lover since she was a child and has spent the past 15 years working with animal shelters and rescue groups trying to make a difference in the lives of abandoned and abused animals. Her home is filled with lovable, wonderful rescued dogs and cats, most with special needs.